COME INTO HIS PRESENCE

SONGS OF WORSHIP FOR SOLO PIANO

ISBN 0-634-06325-1

HAL•LEONARD®
CORPORATION
7777 W. BLUEMOUND RD. P.O. BOX 13819 MILWAUKEE, WI 53213

IN ASSOCIATION WITH

INTEGRITY
MUSIC.

Visit Hal Leonard Online at
www.halleonard.com

ABOVE ALL

Words and Music by PAUL BALOCHE
and LENNY LeBLANC

Pensively

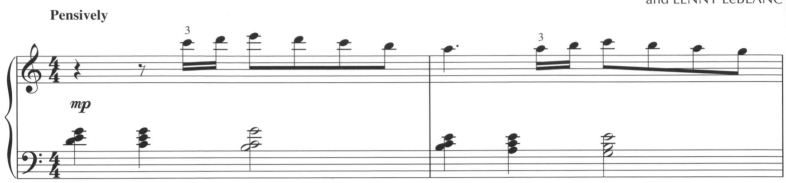

BLESSED BE THE
LORD GOD ALMIGHTY

Words and Music by
BOB FITTS

Moderately

8

COME INTO HIS PRESENCE

Words and Music by
LYNN BAIRD

BREATHE

Words and Music by
MARIE BARNETT

Gently

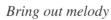

Bring out melody

DRAW ME CLOSE

Words and Music by
KELLY CARPENTER

Moderately slow

With pedal

Bring out melody

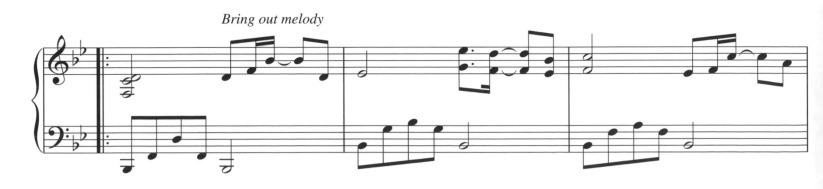

GIVE THANKS

Words and Music by
HENRY SMITH

22

GOD WILL MAKE A WAY

Words and Music by
DON MOEN

JESUS, NAME ABOVE ALL NAMES/ BLESSED BE THE NAME OF THE LORD

Smoothly, not too slow

With pedal

JESUS, NAME ABOVE ALL NAMES
Words and Music by NAIDA HEARN

BLESSED BE THE NAME OF THE LORD

Words and Music by DON MOEN

LORD HAVE MERCY

Words and Music by
STEVE MERKEL

Moderately slow, in 2

mp

With pedal

mf

34

36

MORE PRECIOUS THAN SILVER

Words and Music by
LYNN DeSHAZO

Warmly

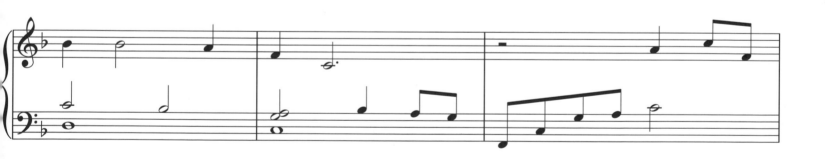

OPEN THE EYES OF MY HEART

Words and Music by
PAUL BALOCHE

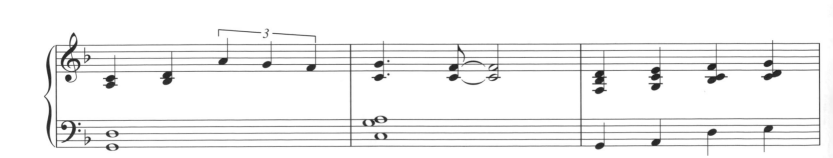

SHOUT TO THE LORD

Words and Music by
DARLENE ZSCHECH

48

D.S. al Coda

CODA

rit.